Parenting With Science: Behavior Analysis Saves Mom's Sanity

Leanne Page, M.Ed., BCBA

CONTENTS

INTRODUCTION

"We can't change our kids…but we can change the things around them to encourage positive behavior change."

Since becoming a mom, I've felt like my brain has turned to mush. I'm pretty sure part of it has. Scientists- where is the research on mommy mush brain? I'm POSITIVE it's a thing.

In another lifetime, I spent my days managing a center that provided ABA therapy for children with autism and other developmental disabilities. I ate, slept, and breathed Applied Behavior Analysis. I provided direct services to kiddos, worked with parents, trained ABA therapists, and consulted with schools. I worked hard, got peed on regularly doing toilet training and had a killer black eye 3 weeks before my wedding. I wore my badges of ABA therapy with pride.

As a Board Certified Behavior Analyst (BCBA), I probably should still be immersed in my field. I am more immersed in dirty diapers, sleep schedules, making homemade baby food (what possessed me to start this trend in our home?), and singing 'Itsy Bitsy Spider'.

Well, it's time my two worlds combined- I present to you my thoughts on bringing ABA to the world of Stay at Home Moms and all Moms of Littles.

ABA has been proven through peer- reviewed research to be an effective intervention for ALL kinds of populations, not just for children with disabilities. ABA WORKS. It just works. For everyone.

ABA has been proven to work with just about any population or group you can think of: kids with disabilities, kids and adults with autism spectrum disorders, people in prison (seriously), alcoholics, weight-challenged folks (ahem, me post-baby), dogs, penguins, any animals, and the list goes on and on.

ABA works for everyone- even the Littles who have taken over your home, your time, your sanity.

As Moms, we see and read all kinds of things from sleep training to how to introduce solid foods to potty training. These methods and theories are pretty much never backed by science or research yet everyone gets all up in arms about them.

I only want to present scientifically proven methods to increase positive behaviors by modifying environmental events. In plain English: we can't change our kids' behaviors, but we can change the things around them to encourage positive behavior change.

The strategies presented here are research-based (see the bibliography if you don't believe me). They are positive behavior supports and are not individualized, targeted behavior interventions. If your child needs an individual behavior intervention plan, please find a BCBA in your area. Contact the Behavior Analysis Certification Board (www.bacb.com).

Me- I'm sharing the global stuff. The big picture ideas that have been proven to WORK! I want you to be able to encourage good behaviors, then catch your kiddos being good and reinforce those behaviors. I want your life to be just a little bit easier as a result!

I'm particularly talking to you, beloved SAHMs and Moms of Littles. You are my people now. Let's stick together in our sweatpants and headbands. Let's join forces and use research-based strategies to improve our everyday lives! Let's share in those successes together! We can do this!

DISCLAIMERS

"If you are not a mom, then just imagine your name every time you see the word Mom in this book."

In this world of lawsuits, hurt feelings, and trophies for everyone, I feel the need to give a few disclaimers.

1. If you have a child with severe behavior problems that are impacting your daily life, please find a Board Certified Behavior Analyst to create an individualized behavior intervention plan for you. Contact the Behavior Analyst Certification Board. You can find more information at bacb.com.

2. Even though I speak specifically about Littles throughout this book, these strategies are good for everyone. ABA works for any and all populations! Check out my bibliography to see the research behind that statement. If you have Bigs in your household and maybe would appreciate a book targeted at your people, let your voice be heard at parentingwithaba.org. Maybe I can put a little something together for you. For now, just adapt these examples.

3. Moms. Throughout this book, I am speaking to Moms. That's because Moms are my people. We are a tribe and we must stick together. Does that mean that Dads can't implement these strategies? Grandma, caregiver, babysitter? No of course not, silly. If you are not a Mom, just imagine your name every time you see the word Mom in this book.

4. These are positive behavior supports. These are antecedent interventions. What that means is they are designed to prevent problem behaviors, not serve as consequences. The idea is to prevent problem behavior and create opportunities for your child to succeed. Then catch your Littles (or Bigs) being good and reward them for it! Win-win!

Leanne Page

1
WHAT IS POSITIVE REINFORCEMENT?

"Don't waste your time on random rewards."

It means praising your kid, right? Maybe giving them a treat or a reward? Is it when you cheer them on at t-ball?

By definition, positive reinforcement occurs when something is presented immediately following a behavior. As a result, that behavior occurs more often in the future.

Behavior→Something is added/given→behavior occurs more often in the future

Randomly giving out praise, candy, stickers, tokens, rewards, does not equal positive reinforcement.

Being positive towards your child, being encouraging, being their best cheerleader does not necessarily equal positive reinforcement. What the what?!

There are two key points here:

1. Immediately following the desired behavior
2. An increase in the desired behavior

Your kid does a good job sitting nicely through dinner at a restaurant so the next day you take him to the park---what is the problem here? It's not immediate.

Your kid does a good job sitting nicely through dinner at a restaurant so you give him ice cream. Next time you go to a restaurant your meal is a disaster and your Little is all over the place---what is the problem here? The desired behavior didn't increase.

If your kid goes in the potty and you praise the heck out of them only for her to have an accident an hour later---was your praise a strong enough reinforcer? No. The desired behavior didn't increase.

As a mom, what does this technical definition have to do with you? You don't have time to read jargon or mumbo jumbo. You have Littles to feed, bathe, entertain, keep alive. I hear you!

It's easy. Just pay attention to what happens after you give what you consider a reward. Was it effective? Did the desired behavior increase? Nope- then it's time to go back to square one. Make the reward immediate and make it strong enough that the behavior will increase in the future.

Good examples:

Your child eats all the food on their plate at dinner. You give lots of praise and extra screen time after dinner. The next night, they eat all their food again! (Hint: give the same positive reinforcement so this trend of peaceful family dinners continues.)

Your child picks up their toys the first time you ask them to. You give them a marble in their marble jar to help them earn a big reward. Next time the toys are out- your child cleans up without protest. A Mom's dream come true!

Positive reinforcement in action!

Another tip- make sure the size of the reinforcer matches the size of the action. What in the world does that mean? If your child says "thank you", does that warrant a trip to Disneyland? I don't think so. On the opposite end, if your child eats a whole plate of vegetables, a "good job" might not be enough.

If the behavior takes a lot for your kiddo to do, make sure the reward is a little bigger. If the behavior is easy peasy, then maybe don't go overboard with the praises and lavish gifts.

Think of "make the punishment fit the crime". Only do the opposite. We want to avoid ever needing to use punishment. Make the reinforcer fit the action.

Take away- don't just give your kid candy and stickers and whatnot willy nilly. Take a minute to think about what you are doing and pay attention to what happens next time in the same situation. Make the reward fit the behavior.

Remember- give the reinforcer immediately after the good behavior. Pay attention to whether it actually increases that good behavior next time!

Don't waste your time on random rewards. Take the time to effectively use positive reinforcement!

Positive Reinforcement	
Goal:	Use rewards efficiently and effectively to increase positive behavior. Quit wasting time!
Steps:	1. Good behavior occurs. 2. Give something to the child- praise, sticker, token, etc. 3. Make sure the behavior increases in the future.
Tips:	- Pay attention to whether the behavior increases in the future. - Give the positive reinforcement immediately. - Make the size of reinforcement match the behavior.

2
PAIRING

"Stick with it until the less desirable activity is no longer an issue in your home."

When working in schools as a special education teacher, I heard a lot about 'pairing' when you first start working with a child. This meant to pair myself with reinforcement so the student would find me reinforcing (and not hate my guts as their new teacher). At first, I would just play with the student and give them access to all the best reinforcers. That way they would see the teacher as someone awesome who lets you play with toys instead of just that bossy lady in the nerdy clothes. I'm way less nerdy now as a BCBA and stay at home mom. Yeah, right.

ABA therapists often appear to be the most bubbly, exciting people ever when they first start working with a new client. Over time, parents may notice that this extreme enthusiasm fades as the child learns to work with that person. The therapist isn't going through mood swings- it's intentional. Most of the time at least.

As a mom, you yourself should already be reinforcing to your child and you don't have to try to make your presence in their life reinforcing to them. I mean- we do meet their every need. All day long. Every day. 24/7. EVERY need. Hopefully, you do play with your kids and they like playing with you, too!

Anyway- the idea of 'pairing' can be useful to us Moms of Littles when we think about everyday activities that must happen but are not always super reinforcing to our children. We are trying to transfer the reinforcing properties of the fun thing to whatever is less desirable to your kiddos. Just like I would pair myself with reinforcement, you can pair an activity with reinforcement to make it less stressful.

What things do your kids avoid, protest, and make a living nightmare for you? Getting dressed, eating vegetables, taking turns, etc? If we try to pair these things with something reinforcing, then we can decrease problem behaviors that happen during everyday routines. Over time, the reinforcing properties will transfer to that activity and it won't be an issue any longer! Woo-hoo!

Think back to the definition of positive reinforcement- it has to increase the likelihood of the desired behavior in the future. I'm not talking about throwing out candy during every un-fun routine or activity.

Pay attention to the specifics- is it just carrots or is it all vegetables that cause screaming and gnashing of teeth? Is it putting on jeans or all pants that leads to a child face down on the floor claiming their legs are broken and they can't possibly put on pants? Does your toddler scream at everyone or just Mom?

Let's look at some examples:

Example 1: Your kid hates putting on their shoes but loves singing songs. Reserve the favorite songs for when you are putting on their shoes. I know you are dying to sing (insert most annoying kid song title here), but don't do it except when it's time to put on shoes.

Your response: That will never work!

Me: Oh just try it. Research shows that combining a less preferred activity with a highly preferred activity can decrease problem behaviors. It can increase the likelihood of your child engaging in the less preferred activity without protest.

Me: What have you got to lose?

Example 2: You want your child to engage in conversation with you, but they don't really like talking. Well, talk about their preferred items or activities while DOING their preferred activities. Watch 'Frozen' together. Again. But actually watch it this time and talk about what is going on in the movie. Maybe even hit the pause button and chat for a minute. That quiet kid may be ready to open up all about Princess Elsa

Example 3: Your kid hates eating vegetables but loves being outside. Why not have dinner on the patio? Oh yeah, snow, rain, hail, tornadoes, blistering heat. Well, when the weather is nice, eat those veggies outside! If the weather is horrendous, maybe you can move their seat near a window and look outside. It's better than nothing!

Example 4: Your kid only plays with trains and it's making you crazy. You need more variety in your life than Thomas can really offer. Pair something with trains. Every single time a train comes out of the toy bin- Oh who am I kidding- every time a train comes off the floor that is littered with toys. When a train comes off the floor, then it's also time to play with _____(blocks, crayons, bubbles, whatever)__. Trains cannot be played with unless the other thing is out too. You can incorporate the two activities: build a tunnel for the train out of the blocks, pop the bubbles with the train, color pictures of trains, whatever you can come up with. Over time, the new activity will be reinforcing without the train and you now have two things to play with your sweet Little. Or two things to listen to them play with while you make dinner, vacuum, dust, and do laundry all at the same time.

Example 5: Suddenly your toddler hates bath time. What? This used to be really fun time but these days being wet is so terrifying, the child must screech like rabid hyenas are attacking them. Well, what is your kid into right now? Trucks? Okay- let's get a water safe truck toy that is only for bath time. If you want to play with the special truck, then you have to get wet and clean in the tub. The special truck toy cannot come out any other time- he lives in the tub.

Shall I go on?

A real example from my life for even infants: my Little baby was having a hard time taking a bottle a) at bedtime and b) from someone other than me. We paired the bedtime bottle with a few minutes of watching 'The Wiggles'. Soon she let her dad feed her before bed regularly and I didn't worry about her going to bed with an empty stomach and waking me up in the middle of the night because she was hungry. It was a win-win. Plus, my husband did a mean rendition of the song 'Fruit Salad'. What's not to be happy about? We faded out the show and just combined bedtime bottle with TV when we wanted to.

Big picture- fade out the highly preferred activity over time. You don't have to keep pairing these things forever. When it feels like you are having a lot of successes, then start fading out. Don't just drop it all at once. Slow and steady wins the race.

Fading: for the bath example- maybe truck comes out after all the soap is rinsed off and it is playtime. Then truck only comes out at the end of bath, then only every other bath time, etc.

Fading: for the shoes and singing example- you only sing the first verse of a song, then you just hum the song, then you only sing every once in a while at shoe time. You get the idea. I hope.

Pair a less desirable activity with something you know your kid likes. Stick with it until the less desirable activity is no longer an issue in your home.

Pairing	
Goal:	Make an un-fun routine or activity more reinforcing
Steps:	1. Pick a specific routine or activity that often leads to problem behavior. 2. Every single time you do that routine, combine it with something your kid likes- a song, activity, a toy, etc. 3. Over time, the problem routine should become more reinforcing. 4. Eventually, fade out the paired preferred activity and revel in your success!
Tips:	- Just pick one routine at a time. - Pair it with the fun thing EVERY time to speed up the process! - Save the fun thing for only when you need it. Make it extra special. - Don't forget about this strategy- try it with something different someday!

Leanne Page

3
FIRST, THEN

"Go You! Go evidence-based practices! It's a win-win."

First do your homework, then you can play Wii.

First eat your vegetables, then you can have a cookie. (Or Bark Thins in my case. Have you seen these amazing culinary concoctions? Dark chocolate with pumpkin seeds and sea salt. It will change your life. I eat waaay more vegetables now so I can have it!)

First do your job, then get a paycheck.

First convince your baby to take a nap, then collapse onto the floor.

First put on clean clothes, then go shopping.

First sit at the table, then you can eat.

First wash your hands, then you can play with toys.

First put on your shoes, then we go play outside.

The list could (and does) go on and on.

First_____, then _____.

This natural first do one thing to earn something fun is something you already do every day in your parenting. It just happens. You may not even think about it and you probably don't say it out loud.

But what if you did? Say it out loud? To your kids? Tell them what the logic is and what good thing is coming to them? What if you used this natural occurrence on purpose?

Here is a good natural example where verbalizing the principle might prevent problem behavior.

Your 2-year-old is playing with a toy and it's time to go somewhere. You pick him up and take him to the car. In order to get him in the car seat, you take the toy out of his hand but plan to put it right back in his hands after you get him buckled.

Option 1: Just take the toy, buckle the kid, and ignore his protests, however loud they may be.

Option 2: As you are getting to the car say, "First get buckled, then get your toy." Do the same actions as above but the kid knows he is getting his toy back so hopefully he isn't struggling against you. You get him buckled faster and avoid some un-fun 2-year-old behavior.

Using the consistent language of "First _____, then _____" lets your child know that something good is coming and that they have some control over the situation. They can choose to engage in that first behavior (do your homework, get buckled in the car, eat your veggies, wash your hands) in order to get the *then* thing promised to them.

In the special education and behavior therapy world, we often do this with visuals.

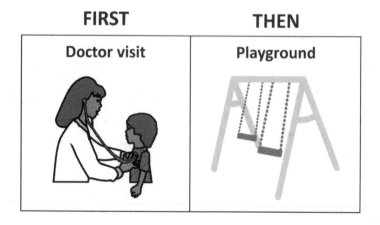

If you find something like that is necessary for the hardest parts of your daily routine, add pictures! Maybe you need one in the bathroom for "First brush your teeth, then book time." Maybe you need one in your laundry room for yourself that says "First fold the clothes, then get on Facebook."

You don't have to constantly be telling your child what is next. "First get out of bed, then brush your teeth. First put on clean clothes, then go downstairs. First sit at the table, then eat breakfast. First get your backpack, then get in the car….." That's cray cray. You'd sound even more like a broken record than you do now. Did you think that was even possible?

Reserve this language for the times when you need to *prevent* problem behavior. Use it when your kid could use an extra hint or two in order to stay out of trouble and follow directions. You know when those times are for your child and you probably already have a plan in your mind to reward them for behaving through those hard times.

Say it out loud. Let the kid know what he/she gets for the 'then'. It's great that you have an idea or a plan in your mind- does your Little know this? Or are they assuming the very worst? Mean mommy is never going to let me do anything fun! Let them know that something good is coming- you just have to do something specific first to earn it!

Keep it simple. First _(do action)_, then __(get something)__. Get something might mean get to do something. I'm not saying give your kid candy every time they do a desired action. Maybe they just get a high five. "First pick up your toys, then high five!" If it works, it works. "First put on your shoes, then we can listen to Uptown Funk." Whatever!

What you're doing is a research-based strategy called The Premack Principle. You are so smart. You've been doing it all along and now you have a name for it! Go You! Go evidence-based practices! It's a win-win.

First use the Premack Principle, then feel good about yourself and your parenting. And give yourself a treat. Dark chocolate with pumpkin seeds, anyone?

Premack Principle	
Goal:	Decrease problem behavior by using First, Then language and/or visuals
Steps:	1. Pick a specific routine or activity that often leads to problem behavior. 2. Every single time you do that routine let the child know what is coming next. 3. Always use the same language, "First _____, then _____." 4. Provide positive reinforcement for doing desired behaviors!
Tips:	- Be consistent with your wording. - Let your kid know what is coming next as far as possible reinforcers or just what is next on the agenda. - Use the "First, Then" language anytime, for any routine/behavior/etc!

4
SETTING UP THE ENVIRONMENT

"We cannot crawl into their tiny minds and somehow force them to comply with our every wish."

A very scaled down version of the scientific definition of behavior (Johnston & Pennypacker) states: "...that portion of an organism's interaction *with its environment...*"

Behavior does not occur in a vacuum. It's all about the environment. We cannot physically change our children's behavior. We cannot crawl into their tiny minds and somehow force them to comply with our every wish. We cannot control their adorable little bodies like marionettes. So what options are we left with?! Ludicrous!

We can change their environment. We can change the consequences of their behavior and we can modify or change the antecedents to their behavior, or the things that happen *before* a problem behavior occurs. We can set things up in a way to encourage desired behaviors to occur.

Believe it or not, we do have control of our physical homes. It sure doesn't feel like it when you have an army of Littles (one counts as an army sometimes) destroying all your housework. You are the adult and you technically are in control. For real.

A simple technique to increase a specific desired behavior is to *physically* set up the environment to prompt that behavior to occur. Set the conditions just right and watch what your Little can do!

Think about when you throw a party- do you want people traipsing all over your house or do you want everyone together in one spot visiting? So do you spread the food out all over the place or have all food and drinks in one area where you anticipate people will congregate? You already use this strategy without even realizing it!

I put fruit out on the counter each morning as snack suggestions for myself and the good stuff- ahem, dark chocolate- stays stored away behind closed doors. I am attempting to set up my environment to help me be successful at making healthy choices.

Here are a few ideas of how arranging the environment can help you to win at parenting.

Example 1: Language

You want your child to request things politely instead of grabbing or taking them? Put preferred items out of their reach. Only provide these toys or items when they request correctly. Teach them how to request, prompt them to request, give all the support they need, but no more free access without practicing good communication skills!

Example 2: Mobility

Until she was 10 months old, my sweet girl crawled with her face on the ground and one hip up to the sky. I really can't describe it. But we tried doing to encourage her to be more mobile (what is wrong with me?! Having her stationary was a good thing for Mom!). We would put her most favorite items a little farther and farther away from where she was playing so she had to move to get to them. What was the best thing to put far away for her to crawl to? A dog. Our pets and their wagging tails were the best motivators. I would convince them to lay in a certain spot (dog treats are helpful) and baby girl would crawl to them to grab their tails.

Example 3: Food/eating

You are having battles at dinnertime. In order to get your child to eat more of the food you have prepared at mealtime, make sure snack foods aren't available all the time. Restrict access to all foods, especially the most preferred ones, until it is mealtime. Physically make it so your kid can't get to the good stuff until it's time to sit and eat a meal and be sure to include the good stuff as part of the meal or a reward for finishing the meal. You can get locks for fridges and pantry doors in the baby proofing section of a store if you need to go that far. Or maybe I should do that for myself- it's cheaper than joining a diet program. Hmmm.

Example 4: Interrupting

Your child constantly interrupts you. Teach them what you want them to do instead (replacement behavior coming up in a later chapter), such as placing their hand on your arm and looking up at you. Whenever they do this correctly, get down on their level and really look them in the eye and listen to whatever it is they have to say. You don't have to rearrange your home, but you are changing the physical consequences of the appropriate behavior. Physically get down to be eye to eye with them any time they interrupt you appropriately.

Example 5: Social skills

Your kids like to play video games or watch TV and you want them to do more social activities, like play together. Make it so the TV cannot be turned on by your children. My techie husband can figure this out or just hide the remote or take the batteries out. Introduce new collaborative activities- have a big puzzle, craft project, or game sitting out when they get home from school and the remote controls locked away somewhere.

Example 6: Sharing

Do a fun activity with your kids, but only have one paintbrush when painting or not enough game pieces in the game. Make it so you all HAVE to share to be successful at the activity. This also covers turn-taking and maybe even requesting nicely if you have them ask for the shared item.

Think about what behavior you want to INCREASE. Then think of how to set things up to make it easy for that behavior to happen. How can you arrange your environment to INCREASE desired behavior?

Side effect: a decrease in problem behavior. Whoop whoop!

From the father of Applied Behavior Analysis, B.F. Skinner: "The environment shapes people's actions."

Setting up the Environment	
Goal:	Prevent problem behavior through environmental manipulation.
Steps:	1. Identify a behavior you want to increase 2. Physically set up the environment to prompt that behavior to happen. 3. Reinforce the desired behavior!
Tips:	- Be creative. - Think about what your child needs access to in order to be successful. - Don't be afraid to move things in your home, limit access to things, or change up your everyday routine. It's worth it if it increases the good behavior and decreases the bad!

5
TASK ANALYSIS

"What if you could do something, anything, to be able to stop this incessant nagging you hear coming out of your own mouth?"

Do you sound like a broken record? Do you find yourself saying the same things over and over to get your child to complete daily routines? Go wash your hands, don't forget the soap! Did you brush your teeth? Did you use toothpaste? Did you wipe? Did you refill Mommy's wine glass? (Just kidding on the last one. Go refill it yourself. Don't be lazy.)

What if you could do something, anything to be able to stop this incessant nagging you hear coming out of your own mouth?

What if you could use visual supports, either pictures or just written lists, to lessen the amount of time you spend repeating yourself each day?

A task analysis involves breaking a complex skill into smaller, teachable units, the product of which is a series of sequentially ordered steps or tasks. (Cooper, Heron, & Heward, 2007)

More simply, in a task analysis you break down all the steps in the correct order for the routine or activity. Instead of saying them out loud over and over and over and over every day, you write them out or draw them out (hello, clip art and google image search).

Hang this visual up where the activity takes place. Don't put the tooth brushing task analysis in the child's bedroom- put it by the sink where they actually brush their teeth.

Just hanging up a pretty picture isn't going to instantly make your child more independent- you have to teach them to use it. Talk through it first and discuss each step and what comes next. Then practice using it together. Don't say your normal reminders- just point to each step as your child completes it and praise for each step completed correctly.

Once they are able to do all steps on their own- give lots of praise and positive reinforcement to increase that independent behavior in the future!

What types of routines do you do every day that involve nagging on your part? Could you break them down into the component steps and try using a visual task analysis?

Some examples:

- ∞ Brushing teeth

- ∞ Getting dressed

- ∞ Morning routine before pre-school, daycare, school, etc.

- ∞ Taking a bath (supervised, of course)

- ∞ Going potty

- ∞ Making a phone call

- ∞ Washing hands

- ∞ Setting up a certain activity or game

- ∞ Making yourself a snack

- ∞ Changing baby's diaper so Mommy can have a break…one can wish, right?

Example of a picture schedule/ task analysis using pictures for taking a bath:

Brushing Your Teeth

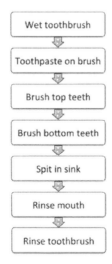

If your kiddo is a reader, just jot down a list on a piece of scratch paper. It doesn't have to be a big fancy work of art. It just needs to be a guide to help your Little complete tasks more independently.

To increase buy-in from your Little, make the task analysis (list or picture schedule) together. Ask- "What steps do you need to do when you go to the bathroom by yourself? Let's find some pictures to show those steps!"

You could also make it a checklist where the little darlings check off each step as they complete it. If your kid is anything like me- adding things to my to-do list after they are done just so I can cross them off- this might give them an extra sense of accomplishment!

Don't bother making lists, picture schedules, you name it with routines your household is handling well. It's for the areas/times of day/ routines where Mama is just exhausted from having to hold hands and remind constantly. Use it where you need it.

Over time, you'll find you don't need it anymore and can get rid of it for that routine. You can make a big deal out of taking it down and celebrating your kids' independence!

Just don't let my Little be too independent. Mama still needs some snuggles, please.

Task Analysis	
Goal:	Help your Little be successful at regular routines, sans all the nagging from Mom
Steps:	1. Identify the most problematic regular routine or activity. 2. Write out all the steps for it. 3. Review the steps with your Little- possibly illustrate. 4. Teach your child to use the checklist or picture schedule. 5. Provide positive reinforcement as they do more and more of the steps independently while using the checklist. 6. Eventually, fade out the use of the task analysis when your kiddo is successful!
Tips:	- Don't include too many steps. Keep it simple. - Include your Little in making the checklist or picture schedule. - Pictures are more fun to look at than reading words. Jazz it up!

Leanne Page

6
TOKEN ECONOMIES

"Little humans do what gets them what they want. They behave in a certain way to achieve a certain outcome."

As moms, we want our kids to want to have good behavior. They should *want* to behave because it's the right thing to do, right? Yeah right.

Have you met a 3 year old with an innate desire to good for this world? It's in there somewhere but at age 3, it's more like threenager-ville. Little humans do what gets them what they want. They behave in a certain way to achieve a certain outcome.

That's a super important point. I'm going to say it again because it's kind of confusing. They behave in a certain way to achieve a certain outcome.

A threenager is likely to tantrum to get access to their favorite toy, TV show, candy, a left shoe they can see on the other side of the room- you name it. They are acting a certain way (tantrum) to achieve a certain outcome (getting whatever random and bizzaro thing they want).

What can we do about this? Is there any way to teach them to behave?! How will we survive the terrible twos, threes, etc.? Well- we can make sure they get what they want not by having a tantrum, but by engaging in desired behaviors.

We can use positive reinforcement in a more structured and specific way than just handing out praise and rewards willy-nilly.

We call this: a token economy.

The definition of a token economy is: 'a behavior change system consisting of three major components: (a) a specified list of target behaviors; (b) tokens or points that participants receive for emitting the target behaviors; and (c) a menu of backup reinforcer items.'

Token economies can possibly take the form of sticker charts, chore charts, marble jars, etc. You need a physical token that your child can earn when they engage in the desired behavior. You do NOT need to go out and spend $50 at the nearest school supply store making a big fancy chart. You can draw 5 circles on a piece of paper. When they do the desired behavior, draw a check mark in the circle. Done. Grab that piece of junk mail off the kitchen counter and a half-eaten, I mean half-broken, crayon.

The next step is to define the behaviors. Again- you don't need a big fancy behavior analytic dictionary. Just pick one to three behaviors that will earn the tokens. You need your Little to understand these. They can't be big grown up ideas like 'being responsible' or 'showing respect'. What does that mean to a Little? Be specific. You earn a token for: (1) following instructions without yelling; (2) eating 5 bites of every food Mom puts in front of you; and (3) putting on your shoes when instructed to.

Pick your battles. You may have a list of 20+ things your Little could stand to improve. I'm pretty sure I have a list of 20+ things to put myself on a token economy. Let's prioritize and make it understandable by the kiddo.

Lastly- what can they earn with these tokens? You can give choices before earning and they can decide at the beginning or in the end. You can make a fancy menu of reinforcers- Chuck E Cheese is the perfect example of this. This many tickets = this super awesome toy.

Or you can just say: get all the stickers, get 5 check-marks, get 10 marbles and earn a fun activity. You can pick from: extra screen time, a trip to the library, a new toy from the dollar spot, etc.

All of that in short form:

1. Pick 1-3 behaviors and make sure your Little understands what they are.
2. Have an actual token they can earn and set a goal.
3. Provide the reward when they reach that goal. Make it a big deal!

When you first start out, set the goal low. If it's too hard to achieve, that won't motivate anyone, especially a Little who is struggling with those behaviors to begin with.

Over time, raise the goal. Make the reward bigger for a bigger goal, smaller for a smaller goal. Play with it to see what is successful for your Little and doable for you in your busy day.

Make every token earned a big deal- lots of praise and excitement.

Don't spend a lot of time and money setting up a fancy system. Like all things we do as parents- as soon as we get a good system down, our Little changes things up on us and we have to be flexible.

Be creative!

∞ My aunt gave this idea from her life: She had a picture of a poodle and her daughter glued cotton balls on it. When she filled the picture, they actually got the poodle!
∞ My sister let her oldest pick out his marbles for a marble jar on a special shopping trip to the craft store (less than $5- don't go crazy folks!). That helped him buy into the process from the get go.
∞ Cut up a picture of the reward like a puzzle. They get a puzzle piece as a token for doing the specific behaviors you identified. The finished puzzle earns the reward!

∞ Look in the app store. Seriously- there are apps for reward charts.

∞ Google 'behavior chart'. You'll find a gazillion cute templates if that's what you're into- cutesy.

∞ I once made a necklace for a student who was really into jewelry. It was a laminated sticker chart necklace and she LOVED it.

∞ You can use play money. I have a friend who gave her daughter play quarters and she exchanged them for dollar bills. Enough dollar bills equaled a big prize! She found a way to teach her child math and economics all at the same time! Genius!

∞ Use magnets on your fridge. Get so many magnets added and you get your reward! Make sure the magnets to be earned are not in a place where little hands could sneak them on there, though.

∞ Make it part of a daily schedule or visual routine such as a task analysis that you learned about in this book. Have the routine written out and get a check mark each day for each step of the routine. So many checks across so many days equal fun times!

∞ Punch cards. You can buy these online, but there are also lots of free templates out there. You use a hole punch like a frequent shopper card. You could make your own but just google it. They're all over the internet- Behavior Punch Cards.

∞ Tie in their favorite character or subject of interest. You can make an Elsa behavior chart, or make the boxes in the shape of train tracks for Thomas fans!

Here's a sample for your viewing enjoyment:

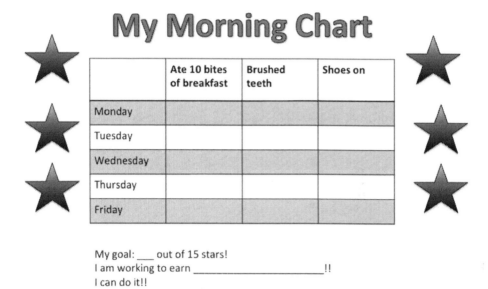

My Morning Chart

	Ate 10 bites of breakfast	Brushed teeth	Shoes on
Monday			
Tuesday			
Wednesday			
Thursday			
Friday			

My goal: ___ out of 15 stars!
I am working to earn _____!!
I can do it!!

One last thought: Someday you will find that things are going well and the token economy goes by the wayside. Remember it when a new problem behavior crops up and you are once again at your wit's end. Start over. Pick new behaviors, new rewards, same system.

Token Economies

Goal:	Create a structured reinforcement system to reward desired behaviors
Steps:	1. Identify 1-3 behaviors and define them in Little-friendly language. 2. Identify a reward and a goal for number of tokens to earn. 3. Give an actual token for good behaviors. 4. Celebrate the reward when it is earned! 5. Repeat! Raise the goal gradually as your child is more and more successful!
Tips:	- Let your Little pick the reward. - Start with a low goal and raise it as you go. - Give lots of praise for every token. The little steps along the way are a big deal, too! - Have fun with it! - Change things up when you need to- when Little is tired of it, not interested, etc.

7
ERRORLESS LEARNING

"Even the father of behavior analysis, B.F. Skinner said,
'Errors are not necessary for learning'."

Errorless learning means that we don't let our kids make mistakes.
We fully prompt them to prevent them from making the mistake or
we physically change the situation to block the behavior or mistake
from happening.

Umm…that sounds like being a helicopter mom? I thought you were
against the trophies for everyone mentality… Stick with me. I'll
explain how this is a research-based strategy that *can* be appropriate at
specific times.

From the Texas Guide for Effective Teaching (2013): "Errorless
learning offers the following benefits: (1) Minimizes the number of
errors; (2) Increases overall time available for instruction; (3) Reduces
the likelihood that errors will be repeated in the future; (4) Reduces
frustration and the occurrence of inappropriate emotional behaviors
by increasing opportunities for reinforcement."

Even the father of behavior analysis, B.F. Skinner said, "Errors are
not necessary for learning."

That's a lot of ABA mumbo jumbo. Let me try to explain it better
with some pretend conversations. (I spend 90% of my time with a
Little. I have a lot of conversations with the air, myself, the dog, the
wall, you name it. I clearly need more grown up interaction in my life.
Who's in the same boat? Oh yeah, you can't answer. There I go
again…)

You: I want my Little to stop doing _____!!

Me: Well, can you prevent it or block it from happening?

You: My kid is licking her lips so much that her face is chapped.

Me: Put something in her mouth so that tongue can't even reach the chin to cause it to chap. Something appropriate- like a lollipop, a Vitamin C drop, etc.

You: My kid grabs stuff off the shelves at the grocery store. I can't take him anywhere! When am I supposed to shop?

Me: Occupy his hands so that he can't grab stuff. Get a special object that is just for in the shopping cart- tie something special to the handles maybe. If his hands are occupied, he won't throw boxes of mac and cheese haphazardly and cause eye injuries. That's what moms always say, right? You'll poke someone's eye out?

You: My kid keeps ripping everything off the pantry shelves, making a mess and breaking things!

Me: Lock the pantry door. Get a baby safety lock thingie and shut it down.

If you have a situation where you can block or prevent an error or behavior problem from occurring- do IT! You aren't over-prompting if you back off over time. You aren't diminishing their independence.

They are making products these days to help prevent errors, too. Have you seen those markers that only work on the coordinating color books? They prevent the problem behavior of coloring on the walls, the sofa, etc. Unless you are Angelina Jolie with her interesting wedding fashions, you probably don't want your child coloring everywhere so markers like these give you the opportunity to use the strategy of errorless learning. Cool!

I was playing with a sweet boy who was learning his colors. I could ask "What color is this __(car, block, whatever)__?" and every time he answered "RED! GREEN! YELLOOOOOW!". He was very enthusiastic. Well, he was just scrolling through color names and not really differentiating between actual colors. To block those errors and that scrolling, I instead asked, "What color is this? Green." (Or whatever the correct color was.) Then, I was blocking the scrolling and preventing those errors from being reinforced.

If I played with this little guy more often I would continue to provide complete color names, then back off to just "Gr" or the beginning sound(s) until eventually I would not give any prompts at all. Doing it this way, the Little would learn his colors much faster than letting him practice errors and find reinforcement for wrong answers. When he enthusiastically yelled out color names, it was super cute and it would make the listener smile, thus reinforcing this wrong answer.

Another example would be using hand over hand prompting. This might come in handy (get it?) when teaching your baby or Little sign language. Instead of sitting there waiting for an infant to imitate a sign using their fine motor skills, just help them to do it.

Example: Teaching my Little to sign for "more" in an attempt to prevent her from fussing and being cranky when she wants something. During snack time or after finishing her meal of baby food, I'd have puffs or yogurt drops or some other finger food where she could see it, but not reach it. I'd give her one and then ask, "Do you want more?" while modeling the sign. If I just waited for her to sign for more, it would have ended pretty terribly. Instead, I put her hands together in an approximation of the 'more' sign and then immediately gave her another puff. Over time, I backed off the prompting and she learned how to do it on her own. Now she never ever fusses and is a perfect angel. Yeah right. She's actually a human child who just happens to be adorable.

Give your Little reinforcement for desired behaviors and correct answers. Give them options for other things they can do- guide their independence into things that will get them access to reinforcement and they will be independent, OUT of trouble, and happy!

Over time- fade out the prompting; back off the support. Sound familiar? As with most strategies I'm sharing with you, pull back slowly and watch your precious Little learn to be more successful and more independent!

Errorless Learning	
Goal:	Prevent problem behaviors from occurring by blocking them
Steps:	1. Identify the problem behavior
	2. Brainstorm ways you can prevent it from happening
	3. Make changes to the environment or situation to block the problem behavior.
	4. Fade out over time.
Tips:	- Only do this for a specific problem behavior to prevent prompt dependence.
	- Only do it for the amount of time necessary.
	- Provide positive reinforcement for desired behaviors!

8
GROUP CONTINGENCIES

"Can you say positive peer pressure?"

Are you on man-on-man defense or zone? Is it you against one or you against seemingly 1,000?

Do you have multiple Littles or kiddos of any age that tend to band together to form a mutiny in your household? I mean, do you have several adorable children who you dress in precious coordinating outfits and who share perfectly, act like angels, and make your life a breeze? Or do you make it look like that on Facebook at least?

Well, we've reviewed what positive reinforcement really is and how to use a token economy, as well as other pertinent strategies. What if you put those together and make it so ALL members of the household participate together to earn one big reinforcer?

You: Huh?

Me: Oh just wait. This will be totally worth it.

A group contingency means that ALL members of the group must perform the desired behavior for the reward to be granted.

Can you say positive peer pressure?

A group contingency can mean that siblings monitor each others' behavior and support each other to make sure everyone is on the right track and everyone is going to earn the reward/reinforcer.

You probably need a pretty good reinforcer to get all your kiddos to work together for the greater good like this. A trip to Disneyland? Just kidding. A trip to McDonald's just might be enough. Or to the park- even cheaper!

I'm talking about an interdependent group contingency- all members of the group (family) must meet the criteria you set in before anyone gets the reward (Cooper pg 569). If we are getting technical there are other forms of group contingencies but I'll save a more in-depth look for another day.

How to do this?

(1) Decide what the target behaviors are for the contingency. Select no more than 3 behaviors and make them specific so Littles can understand and know exactly what to do! Remember- "making good choices" or "being a good citizen" leaves the door wide open for misconstruing the meaning and your poor Little is left dangling in the breeze, unsure of what exactly their sibling is pressuring them to do! "Listen to Mommy" might leave you with a shadow that feels the need to hear every word out of your mouth. A personal phone call? What's that?

(2) Choose a reinforcer. How about let the kids decide as a group? Give a few choices within your budget- both financial and time budgets- and let them pick! They will already have to work together just to pick one reward! Make the reward powerful enough to get them to buy in without being entirely too over the top like the perfect Pinterest Mom. Staying up past their normal bedtime is way cheaper and easier than a theme party including the whole neighborhood. Be creative.

(3) Set your time period. A month is too long. A day may be too short. What is best for your family? Make it achievable at first- so start smaller than you think necessary. Over time, you can make it longer and longer until a month is achievable for your kiddos. Don't make the time frame so long that your kids lose interest or aren't capable of holding it together to earn the reward.

(4) Start monitoring their behavior and remind them to keep each other on track to earn that big exciting treat of ice cream

for dinner one night! Or whatever kooky thing you can convince them is fun and exciting yet easy and cheap to implement.

Caution: if you have a super bossy kid, maybe this isn't for your family. Or maybe you need to have a chat with Miss or Mr. Bossypants about how to nicely encourage their siblings instead of bossing them around all the time.

This is a great learning opportunity for how to give and receive constructive criticism. Maybe it's a great learning opportunity for how to nicely ask your siblings for help with something. Maybe it's a great learning opportunity for Mom to back off and just watch the kids interact on their own without intervening. I'm looking at you, helicopter Mom. No hovering necessary.

We see group contingencies in schools when teachers have the whole class working together to earn a class party, extra recess, read-a-thon, or what have you.

We see group contingencies in the corporate world when a team is working together to meet a certain goal- maybe a sales goal or a big deadline.

Plusses to using this strategy:

∞ You don't need to come up with separate reinforcement plans for each kid.
∞ Your kids may learn to work together, play together, and communicate better as they try to reach the common goal.
∞ You and your spouse/partner/significant other can be on the same page with a structured reinforcement system so the kids know exactly what is expected from all caregivers.
∞ Parents can back off a little and not be all up in their kiddos' business all the time.

Get the family all working together to earn something awesome and see an increase in desired behaviors in your daily routine!

Group Contingencies	
Goal:	All family members work together for a common reward
Steps:	1. Pick 1-3 specific target behaviors. 2. Pick a powerful reinforcer and decide when it will be given. 3. Watch your kids help (peer pressure) each other to have good behavior! 4. Give that reward!!
Tips:	- Make sure it is achievable at first. - Watch out for bossy britches. - Use a powerful reinforcer as the reward. - Make it a fun game!

9
REPLACEMENT BEHAVIOR

"What CAN they do? What IS a good choice?"

Make it STOP! Stop the crying. Stop the tantrums. Stop the arguments. Stop the power struggles. Stop, stop, stop!

We often talk about disciplining our children and getting them to stop doing bad behaviors. If we were truly successful in getting our kiddos to stop doing anything outside our perfect expectations, what would we be left with? Robots?

When we want our child to stop doing something, we need to teach them what to do instead. What CAN they do? What IS a good choice?

I like this quote from Snell & Brown (2006), "Teachers and other human services professionals should be in the business of building positive, adaptive repertoires, not merely reacting to and eliminating behaviors they find troublesome."

Isn't this true for parents, too? Shouldn't we be in the business of building our kids up and teaching them the good stuff? Let's teach them the behaviors we DO want to see more of on a daily basis!

In ABA, we call these replacement behaviors. When it's time to reduce a problem behavior, what will replace it? How will the child get his or her needs met? How will they get their point across? How will they communicate, behave, and participate in society?

What will *replace* the problem behavior?

In answering that question, we have to really think about the problem behavior itself. Why is our child screaming at the top of her lungs? Why did our son take his pants off in the middle of Target? What exactly are they trying to achieve by doing these things? How can I give them another option to achieve this?

Coming up with an effective replacement behavior can be hard. This is not your easy, run of the mill Mom stuff. This is your stuff to tackle only *after* having that second cup of coffee. Or third. Whatever.

The new behavior needs to be faster and more efficient in getting the child what he needs or wants. So not only does the replacement behavior need to help them meet their needs- it needs to do it better than the problem behavior does!

Whoa! Did I lose you there? Let's break it down.

Here are some simple examples to start with:

- ∞ Asking for a toy instead of grabbing it
- ∞ Tapping Mom on the arm lightly instead of saying "Mom, Mom, Mom!" at the top of your lungs (Spoken in my best Stewie from Family Guy voice)
- ∞ Walking away from a sibling instead of screaming at them when upset
- ∞ Ask for a different snack instead of dumping yogurt on the carpet

These seem like pretty obvious replacement behaviors to me. Are you with me still? What can your child do INSTEAD of the undesired behavior? It has to achieve your child's desired result.

Here are some harder examples.

- ∞ Waiting. You are in line at the grocery store. Your child doesn't want to wait to get in the car so they suddenly begin to cry. What can you do about it? Teach a replacement behavior. Teach them to ask how much longer. Well- that sounds annoying as a parent. "Are we there yet? Are we there yet?" Teach them to time how long you have to wait on your phone. Or better yet- by counting in their head! When it's your turn, ask them what number they got to and be excited about it. Praise the heck out of them for counting so well and for waiting so nicely! Teach them something to do other than crying that will get your attention and praise and hopefully help pass the time spent waiting.

∞ Tantrums when hungry. Teach them to ask for a snack. This one, you'll need to prompt them to ask for a snack BEFORE it reaches tantrum level. Can you imagine a screaming child and the mom saying, "Now ask for a snack. Say, 'Can I have a snack, please?'". Yeah, that'll go really well. Practice requesting food before the problem occurs. You know when that tantrum is coming. Jump in there ahead of it and prompt your child to request food. What if you don't have a snack on you right then? (Seriously- start packing granola bars in your bag. You are a Mom now.) Then the waiting technique from above would come in handy!

∞ Sibling relationships. Big sister always dictates what game to play, what pretend story to act out, and what television show to watch. Little brother just wants a chance to make the choice, so he hits big sister. Teach him how to request activities with his words and not through violence. Teach him to stand up for himself, say what he wants to do, and then make that happen. Reinforce his requesting by intervening and making sure he gets his way when he asks correctly- at least at first.

∞ Sibling relationships, continued. Other ideas for the above situation: teach little brother to play by himself instead of hitting sister. Teach little brother to come ask you for help instead of hitting sister. Just pick one replacement behavior- but there are lots of options out there!

What do you want them to do INSTEAD of the problem behavior? What do you want to REPLACE the problem behavior?

What CAN your Little do?

How to do it:

∞ Actually teach your child the steps you want them to take. Break it down. Teach it. Talk about it. Practice it. Review it. Do all of these things pro-actively when there are no problem behaviors occurring.

∞ Be straightforward. Tell them "Instead of grabbing the toy, you need to ask for it."

∞ And since we've made it so far in this book together, I really hope you aren't surprised by the last tip: REINFORCE the good behavior! Use positive reinforcement every single time you see that replacement behavior in action.

Reinforce the good. Prevent the bad. Say it with me. Reinforce the good. Prevent the bad. Reinforce the good!

Replacement Behaviors	
Goal:	Teach your child what to do INSTEAD of a problem behavior
Steps:	1. Identify the problem behavior you want to replace. 2. Choose a replacement behavior that will serve the same purpose for your child. 3. Explicitly teach the replacement behavior. 4. Reinforce the replacement behavior every time it happens!
Tips:	- Make sure the replacement behavior is helping your child get whatever they were after in the first place. - Reinforce, reinforce, reinforce. - Be consistent. Help them to use the same replacement behavior every time the situation arises until they can do it on their own.

10
FINDING YOUR OWN REINFORCEMENT

"Here's to YOU!"

A key theme to this whole book has been the effective use of positive reinforcement. We've talked about using positive reinforcement to increase desired behaviors. We've talked about using positive reinforcement efficiently. We've talked about using positive reinforcement for your children. And by we, I mean me. I've talked about all those things and I hope you've been listening.

But what about Mom? Doesn't she deserve a little positive reinforcement? The answer is: YES! YES! YES!

Applied Behavior Analysis is used for corporate management and building successful business- a branch of ABA called organizational behavior management. A big part of this is providing feedback and reinforcement to workers- just like with kids!

If you are a working Mom (or parent), hopefully you are getting performance feedback and reinforcement at your job. At the very least, you are receiving a paycheck to reinforce your behavior of going to work every day!

If you are a Stay at Home Mom, where are you getting your performance feedback and positive reinforcement? Who is giving you the 'paycheck'?

If you are a working Mom, you need reinforcement for both your jobs- your career and your Mom job! You are in the same boat as the Stay at Home Mom. Where are you getting reinforcement for the wonderful job you are doing as a mother?

In a perfect world, your children would always say "thank you" and your husband would walk in the door each evening complimenting the state of your home, the meal you've somehow gotten ready, and how fantastic your children are doing. In the real world, we need to learn to self-reinforce and to put ourselves in a position to receive positive reinforcement from other sources.

Self-reinforcement, huh? How can we provide positive reinforcement for ourselves? Quit talking nonsense.

Legit ideas:

∞ Give yourself a reward for every xx minutes of housework you engage in. If I clean for 45 minutes total, I can sit and watch an episode of Veronica Mars on amazon.
∞ If I fold and put all the laundry away, I can have a Diet Coke.
∞ When I successfully get all Littles to take a nap, I can lay down too. Or shop online. Or get on social media.
∞ When I finish potty training this angel child, I am going to get a babysitter and Mama's going out on the town with the grown ups!
∞ For every 5 pounds I lose, I can buy a new article of clothing.

Build in little rewards for yourself and arrange for breaks from your job as Mom, too. Swap weekend mornings with your husband so you can stay in bed a little longer than usual. Have your mother-in-law come watch the kids so you can have a date night.

You don't have to buy yourself rewards- but arrange for things that can reinforce your behavior. What behavior are you reinforcing? The behavior of being one awesome, bada--, Mom!

Research tells us to select small, easy to administer rewards for ourselves. The world of Applied Behavior Analysis instructs us to use small consequences that can be obtained immediately and frequently. Are you going to reward your kids with a trip to Disney World all the time? Is a spa day really something you can give yourself every week?

(If you get to go to the spa every week just stop reading now. You are not one of us.)

Keep it simple. Do a simple task, earn a small reward that is still pretty good for you. Remember how I mentioned chocolate bark in a previous chapter? Maybe don't always reward yourself with food (ahem, talking to myself here), but give yourself a little something when you deserve it!

An important point from Cooper, Heron, & Heward (2007): "Self-administered reinforcement does not have to be self-delivered: the learner could make a response that results in another person providing the reinforcer."

As a teacher, I taught students to self-evaluate their work or their behavior, then show that to the teacher for feedback and praise. They would seek out that reinforcement with a simple, "Look what I can do!" (Think: Stuart from Saturday Night Live.)

You: Okay- but what does this have to do with Moms? Especially Moms of Littles? Me: Only everything.

We need to find sources who will provide that reinforcer. Who will share in your excitement over your Little eating solid foods without throwing them in your hair? Who will be thrilled over the words "went pee pee in the potty"? Who can you tell about getting 8 hours of sleep in a row even with a house crawling with little people?

Find a tribe. Make your tribe. Surround yourself with people who care about you and understand motherhood- at least a little bit. Find a community of Moms who build you up. Maybe this is your lifelong friends, many of whom have become Moms around the same time as you. Maybe this is a club or group, or class that you've attended. Maybe you have neighbors with Littles. Maybe it's your own mom or your sister or your cousins.

Now that you've found your people- talk tot them! Text them a picture of your kid going down the big slide at the park for the first time. They will be excited about it. They will praise you. And THAT will reinforce your behavior of being a super, fantastic Mom!

Share your good news with your people. Maybe don't post all this on social media- your 'friends' or acquaintances won't care. Sorry to break it to you. Step away from the Facebook. But your real *friends* care. I promise. If they aren't reinforcing you- find someone else to talk to you.

Your Little's grandmothers probably like to hear all the details and successes, even if they seem minor to the outside world. Tell them! Let them praise you for being a great mom! Let them offer to come babysit so you can go shopping by yourself! Take those opportunities to get some of that positive reinforcement!

When someone offers you any sort of help, childcare, a meal, a fun time to interact with real live grown ups, TAKE IT! You need these things to reinforce your behavior. What behavior? Oh yeah- just being a kick a-- Mom.

Play dates, coffee dates, lunch dates, childcare swaps, any hangouts that can provide you access to good conversation- DO IT! These are opportunities for you to be reinforced.

Find your own positive reinforcement. Self- administer rewards by making little deals or contracts with yourself. Put yourself in contact with those who can give you reinforcement.

Most importantly- ask for it. Tell your husband you like to hear from him about how you're doing as a mom. Tell your tribe you need the feedback. Seek out that reinforcement.

You need positive reinforcement. You deserve positive reinforcement. You earn it each day- so go ahead and give yourself some!

Go You!! Keep on being an incredible, amazing, stupendous, super smart Mom! Keep on using positive behavior supports to prevent problem behavior by reinforcing good behavior.

Holy moly, you're a rock star, Mom. Here's to YOU!

GLOSSARY

Applied Behavior Analysis- the process of systematically applying interventions based upon the principles of learning theory to improve socially significant behaviors to a meaningful degree, and to demonstrate that the interventions employed are responsible for the improvement in behavior. (Baer, Wolf, & Risley, 1991)

Antecedent- conditions immediately before a behavior occur; what happens immediately before a behavior occurs.

Behavior- the activity of living organisms; human behavior includes everything that people do. A technical definition: "that portion of an organism's interaction with its environment that is characterized by detectable displacement in space through time of some part of the organism and that results in a measurable change in at least one aspect of the environment." (Johnston & Pennypacker, 1993a)

B.F. Skinner- the father of behavior analysis who studied operant conditioning in the 1970s and published many books including *Verbal Behavior* (1957) and *About Behaviorism* (1974).

Consequence- what happens following a behavior; Technical definition: a stimulus change that follows a behavior of interest. Some consequences, especially those that are immediate and relevant to current motivational states, have significant influence on future behavior; other have little effect (Cooper, Heron, & Heward, 2007).

Errorless learning- a teaching procedure originated by B.F. Skinner in which the teacher prevents the learner from making errors. Correct responding is reinforced and conditions are arranged to prevent errors.

Group contingency- when a contingency to earn a reinforcer is applied to a set group of individuals.

Interdependent group contingency- a contingency in which reinforcement for all members of a group is dependent on each member of the group performing the desired behaviors as outlined in the contingency.

Hand-over-hand prompting- the highest level of prompting; physically guiding another's hands to elicit the desired response; doing the action for the person by holding their hands.

Positive reinforcement- occurs when a behavior is followed immediately by the presentation of a stimulus that increases the future frequency of the behavior in similar conditions (Cooper, Heron, & Heward, 2007).

Premack Principle- high probability behaviors are used to reinforce low probability behaviors. Example: First ____, then _____.

Prompt- an assistance given to help the child engage in desired behavior; can be direct or indirect; can be verbal or physical.

Prompt fading- systematically removing the prompt; slowly increasing the child's independence by decreasing the level and amount of prompting given.

Reinforcer- Responses from the environment that increase the probability of a behavior being repeated (McLeod, 2007).

Replacement behavior- the behavior you teach your child to replace a problem behavior. Must serve the same function & be faster and more efficient in getting the child what he needs or wants.

Stimulus- a thing or event that evokes a specific response. Technical definition: " an energy change that affects an organism through its receptor cells" (Michael, 2004).

Task analysis- breaking a skill or routine down into the specific steps; teaching a skill in smaller component parts.

<u>Token Economy-</u> a system of reinforcement in which the participant earns tokens immediately following the target behavior. Later, those tokens can be exchanged for a backup reinforcer (a bigger reward).

BIBLIOGRAPHY

I don't expect you to take my word on all this. Take it from the experts. These strategies are empirically based as evidenced by all of these peer-reviewed research articles. Check 'em out for yourself! Become a behavior analysis expert in all your spare time, Mom!

Alber, S. R., Heward, W. L., & Hippler, B. J. (1999). Teaching middle school students with learning disabilities to recruit positive teacher attention.Exceptional Children, 65(2), 253-270.

Baer, D.M., Wolf, M.M., & Risley, T.R. (1968). Some current dimensions of applied behavior analysis. Journal of Applied Behavior Analysis, 1, 91-97.

Bailey, Donald B., and Mark Wolery. Teaching infants and preschoolers with disabilities. Prentice Hall, 1992.

Bellack, A. S. (1976). A comparison of self-reinforcement and self-monitoring in a weight reduction program. Behavior Therapy, 7(1), 68-75.

Cooper, J., Heron, T., & Heward, W. (2007). Basic Concepts. In Applied Behavior Analysis(2nd ed.). Columbus: Pearson.

Dixon, M.R., Rehfeldt, R.A., & RAndich, L. (2003). Enhancing tolerance to delayed reinforcers; The role of intervening activities. Journal of Applied Behavior Analysis, 26, 263-266.

Green, G. (1996). Behavioral intervention for autism. In C. Maurice, G. Green, & S. C. Luce(Eds.), Behavioral interventions for young children with autism (pp. 29-42). Austin, TX:Pro-Ed.

Hanley, G., Iwata, B., Roscoe, E., Thompson, R., & Lindberg, J. (2003). Response Restriction Analysis: II. Alteration of activity preferences.JABA, 36(1), 59-76.

Hayes, L. A. (1976). The use of group contingencies for behavioral control: A review. Psychological Bulletin, 83(4), 628.

Heward, W.L. (1980). A formula for individualizing initial criteria for reinforcement. Exceptional Teacher, 1 (9), 7,9.

Homme, L. E.; Debaca, P. C.; Devine, J. V.; Steinhorst, R.; Rickert, E. J. (1963) Use of the Premack principle in controlling the behavior of nursery school children. Journal of the Experimental Analysis of Behavior, Vol 6(4), 544.

Johnston, J.M., & Pennypacker, H.S. (1993a). Strategies and tactics for human behavioral research (2nd ed.). Hillsdale, NJ: Erlbaum.

Kazdin, A. E. (Ed.). (1977). The token economy: A review and evaluation. Plenum Publishing Corporation.

Kazdin, A. E. (1982). The token economy: A decade later. Journal of Applied Behavior Analysis, 15(3), 431-445.

Knapp, T.J. (1976). The Premack Principle in human experimental and applied settings. Behaviour Research and Therapy, Vol 14(2), 133-147.

Ling, S., Hawkins, R. O., & Weber, D. (2011). Effects of a classwide interdependent group contingency designed to improve the behavior of an at-risk student. Journal of Behavioral Education, 20(2), 103-116.

MacDuff, G. S., Krantz, P. J., & McClannahan, L. E. (2001). Prompts and prompt-fading strategies for people with autism. Making a difference: Behavioral intervention for autism, 37-50.

McLeod, S. A. (2007). Skinner - Operant Conditioning. Retrieved from http://www.simplypsychology.org/operant-conditioning.html

Michael, J. (2004). Concepts and principles of behavior analysis (rev. ed.). Kalama-zoo, MI: Society for the Advancement of Behavior Analysis.

Neef, N.A., Mace, F.C., Shea, M.C., & Shade, D. (1992). Effects of reinforcer rate and reinforcer quality on time allocation: Extensions of matching theory to educational settings. Journal of Applied Behavior Analysis, 25, 691-699.

Pigott, H. E., Fantuzzo, J. W., & Clement, P. W. (1986). The effects of reciprocal peer tutoring and group contingencies on the academic performance of elementary school children. Journal of applied behavior analysis, 19(1), 93-98.

Premack, D. (1959). Toward empirical behavior laws: I. Positive reinforcement.Psychological Review, 66(4), 219.

Reitman, D., Murphy, M. A., Hupp, S. D., & O'Callaghan, P. M. (2004). Behavior change and perceptions of change: Evaluating the effectiveness of a token economy. Child & Family Behavior Therapy, 26(2), 17-36.

Rivera, M. O., Koorland, M. A., & Fueyo, V. (2002). Pupil-made pictorial prompts and fading for teaching sight words to a student with learning disabilities. Education and Treatment of Children, 197-207.

Skinner, B. F. (1938). The Behavior of organisms: An experimental analysis. New York: Appleton-Century.

Skinner, B. F. (1953). Science and human behavior. SimonandSchuster.com.

Skinner, B. F., Ferster, C. B., & Ferster, C. B. (1997). Schedules of reinforcement. Massachusetts: Copley Publishing Group.

Smith, B. W., & Sugai, G. (2000). A self-management functional assessment-based behavior support plan for a middle school student with EBD. Journal of Positive Behavior Interventions, 2(4), 208-217.

Snell, M. E., & Brown, F. (2006). Designing and implementing instructional programs. Instruction of students with severe disabilities, 5, 111-169.

Sulzer-Azaroff, B., & Mayer, G. R. (1991). Behavior analysis for lasting change. Holt, Rinehart & Winston.

Terrace, H. S. (1963). Discrimination learning with and without "error." Journal of the Experimental Analysis of Behavior 6, 1-27.

Test, D. W., Spooner, F., Keul, P. K., & Grossi, T. (1990). Teaching adolescents with severe disabilities to use the public telephone. Behavior modification,14(2), 157-171.

Wahler, R.G., and Fox, J.J. (1981) Setting events in applied behavior analysis: Toward a conceptual and methodological expansion, Journal of Applied Behavior Analysis, 14 (3), 327-338.

ABOUT THE AUTHOR

Leanne Page, M.Ed., BCBA, has worked with children with disabilities for over 10 years. She earned both her Bachelor's and Master's degrees from Texas A&M University. Whoop! She also completed graduate coursework in Applied Behavior Analysis through the University of North Texas before earning her BCBA (Board Certified Behavior Analyst) certification in 2011.

She has worked as a special education teacher in all kinds of crazy, I mean unique and wonderful environments including elementary and high school self-contained, inclusion, general education, and resource settings.

Leanne also has managed a center providing ABA services to children in one-on-one and small group settings. She has extensive experience in school consultation and teacher training, parent training, and providing direct services to children and families in a center-based or in-home therapy setting.

Leanne started her website- parentingwithaba.org- while living overseas with her husband and baby girl on a small island in the middle of the Pacific Ocean. In such a remote location, it was difficult to find high quality continuing education opportunities. Her coconut phone just wasn't cutting it.

Her hope is twofold: (1) to make it easy for all those who are utilizing Applied Behavior Analysis to find training opportunities interacting with the research; and (2) to share these great ABA strategies with all Moms- not just those who have children on the autism spectrum.

Leanne is now living in the great state of Texas with her adorable family and continues to share ideas and strategies with all Moms through her website.